TESTIMONIALS

The Courage Advantage is a gift to any leadership team in growth mode. Jill's observations will resonate with ambitious entrepreneurs who are looking to grow in a more effortless way. She teaches you how to change your mindset so that growth becomes second nature for you and your team!

—Gino Wickman
Author of *Traction* and Creator of EOS®

In her new book, *The Courage Advantage*, Jill has distilled the takeaways from hundreds of coaching sessions with entrepreneurs and their leadership teams to reveal the reasons that some teams really fly while others just clunk along. Following Jill's approach and the concepts she introduces in this book, you'll be able to decide your way to success.

—Dan Sullivan, Founder of Strategic Coach

A *great* boss must have the courage to establish a compelling vision and the discipline to keep oneself and others focused on the journey. In this wonderfully written book, Jill Young shares three simple, practical ways to stay the course, have some fun, and get things done! If you enjoyed Jill's first book, *The Earning Advantage: 8 Tools You Need to Get Paid the Money You Want,* get ready for more wisdom from a great coach!

—René Boer, Certified EOS Implementer® and
Co-author of *How to Be a Great Boss!*

At first glance, Bruce Lee and Jill Young wouldn't appear to have many similarities. But both are five-foot-something, overwhelmingly powerful, and their teachings have radically transformed the lives of their clients. If you're looking for that edge, look no further. *The Courage Advantage* is your how-to guide to reignite the courage in YOU and YOUR business.

—Michael Hall, Master Culture Index Consultant

Jill's second book builds on the energetic and creative coaching wisdom she shares in *The Earning Advantage*. Her observational expertise is practical, immediately useful and encourages us to embrace three simple, everyday mindsets. I highly recommend acting on Jill's insights if you want to grow your company.

—Alex Freytag, Certified EOS Implementer® and Author of *Achieve Your Vision*

Jill's new book is full of great tools and strategies. She has been a fabulous coach, forcing me to be focused on my highest and best use and how best to improve my leadership skills. Not only am I getting better, I am happier and more fulfilled!

—Heather Ettinger, Visionary, Fairport Asset Management and Luma Wealth Advisors

Great mix of ideas, practical habits, things that can be implemented right away and an easy read—not too long. Jill gets to the point and she's brought the fun, practical and go-forward mentality that she always does for us. This is NOT just a book you read and put on the shelf...I'll go back to this again and again.

—Stephen Park, Integrator, EZBel Construction

If you want to develop a courageous mindset, read this book! Jill clearly outlines, with intelligence, passion, humor, and practical examples, how you can be a more courageous leader. I'm inspired by reading this, and I'm confident you will be too.

—Shannon Waller, Entrepreneurial Team Strategist
Strategic Coach

Jill Young has written a delightful, easy-to-read book with actionable items on how to have courage as a leader. The examples and concepts Jill shares in *The Courage Advantage* will inspire you to be brave and dare to be different!

—Kristie Clayton, Visionary
FIM (Female Integrator Mastermind)

Jill has packed so much wisdom in her new book, *The Courage Advantage*. Her observations, stories and results speak to all leaders. Whether you are a seasoned or new entrepreneur, leader or manager, there is absolute gold in these pages.

—Bobi Siembieda, Certified EOS Implementer® and
Kolbe Consultant, Conrad Business Results

Jill is real and current, a breath of fresh air in the business world. Just spend 20 minutes reading her book and you quickly realize she "gets it." Her examples are rock solid and thought-provoking. If you want practical, real world ideas without an ounce of theory, you've got to read Jill's book.

—Greg Cleary
Leadership Team Coach at Pinnacle

Jill Young is so inspiring. She is one of the bravest and funniest humans I know! This book highlights her wisdom and her fun approach to coaching. What a gift! Like me, you may struggle with sustaining good habits, or being a bit too serious or overly cautious. This book is guaranteed to take away some of the sweat equity in getting your personal and professional life in order. SWEAT LESS! Start reading.

—Victoria Cabot, Certified EOS Implementer®
Velocity6 Leadership

I truly look forward to making *The Courage Advantage* a part of my library for my clients and people I care about who have intentional passion and drive for becoming their personal best.

—Duane Marshall, Pure Business Results
Certified EOS Implementer®

Obsessed! As I was reading this book, I found myself continuously shaking my head and smirking to myself. I kept asking myself, "Is she reading my mind?" I would recommend this book to anyone who has a business or manages people and is looking to create an awesome culture as well as grow their business.

—Lindsey Harrison, Owner and Visionary
The It Crowd Marketing Agency

Sometimes leaders hit the ceiling and they need someone from the "outside" to be a beacon in the fog. Jill is that person. She has invested considerable time in studying the dynamics of leadership teams. She has a passion for helping leaders improve and she generously shares her insights in *The Courage Advantage*. Jill maps out the steps you can take to develop a courageous mindset with great insight and lots of examples. But don't take my word for it, read the book! You will be glad you did.

—Ron Pyke, owner Ronald A. Pyke, CFO

Jill Young is a high-impact, high-energy dynamo who has personally helped hundreds of leaders and their teams. What sets Jill apart is her ability to relate and connect on so many levels with leaders, peers and fans. She's an amazing listener with a wealth of knowledge and ideas in her arsenal. This book gives beautiful insight into Jill's innovative style, sense of humor and wisdom and is sure to entertain and inform!

—Lorie Clements, Certified EOS Implementer®
Springboard Solutions

Other Books by Jill Young

*The Earning Advantage: 8 Tools You Need to
Get Paid the Money You Want*

*The Thinking Advantage: 4 Essential Steps Your
Team Needs to Cultivate Collaboration, Leverage Creative
Problem-Solving, and Enjoy Exponential Growth*

The
Courage
Advantage

3 Mindsets Your Team Needs to Cultivate Fierce Discipline, Incredible Fun, and a Culture of Experimentation

Second Edition

JILL YOUNG

The Courage Advantage: 3 Mindsets Your Team Needs to Cultivate Fierce Discipline, Incredible Fun, and a Culture of Experimentation
© 2020 by Jill Young. All rights reserved.

Published by Author Academy Elite
PO Box 43, Powell, OH 43065
www.AuthorAcademyElite.com

First edition published June 21, 2019.

Library of Congress Control Number: 2020908858

Softcover: 978-1-64746-281-9
Hardcover: 978-1-64746-282-6
E-book: 978-1-64746-283-3

Also available on audiobook.

To my clients of the past, present, and future.
Thank you for leading your companies with truth,
beauty, and goodness.
It is my honor to be your coach.

CONTENTS

I'M AFRAID THAT...

I'm afraid that if I invest in the company, I'll lose my personal security.

I'm afraid that if I fire John, the clients might follow him.

I'm afraid that if we hire for this new position, I'll lose control of quality.

Have you ever heard yourself or your team members using the phrase "I'm afraid that...?" It's a common yet powerful phrase that often gets overlooked. Its frequent use indicates that most people feel some kind of fear daily. Some are motivated by it; others are debilitated by it. Entrepreneurs feel fear as well; the successful ones use this fear to propel themselves and their companies forward. I've observed that true entrepreneurs are in constant growth mode, and growth means change. But great change, change that really sticks, is more like a constant evolution than a revolution, and living in fear makes that evolution scary instead of exciting.

After facilitating over 500 sessions with leadership teams that were in growth mode, I asked myself, *What causes some teams to thrive in the midst of their evolution and others to painfully struggle?* My observation is that the teams that thrive live in courage rather than in fear. Essentially, they have a Courage Mindset—a courageous way of thinking that fuels the evolution. It's not that they don't feel the fear. They feel the fear and do it anyway, and as they live and work in courage rather than fear, the fear they used to feel turns into excitement for the future.

In the following pages, I've dissected this Courage Mindset for you—the entrepreneur—*and* your leadership team. However, you'll only benefit from this book if you and your team really *want* to make the changes it takes to grow the company. If you don't first want to grow, the fear you feel will disguise itself as reality; it'll scare you into staying conservative and avoiding risk. If you aren't sure why you want to grow, stop reading this book, and go find your purpose! Then, come back, and I'll share some mindsets with you that will help you accelerate your growth!

This book is complete with examples from real companies just like yours and ideas for implementation. You'll find that the mindsets I'll teach you are expressed in three different ways: the courage to have discipline, the courage to lighten up, and the courage to experiment.

But First...Where Do We Start? The Action or the Mindset?

For some people, learning a concept *then* applying it until they are successful really changes their mindset. Other times, the mind needs to change *before* the learning takes place.

For example, when I was younger, I took piano lessons. I dreaded the short walk each Saturday to my piano teacher's house, and I dreaded practicing every day. Because I was obedient, I did practice, though I never progressed past the level of a novice. Even though I went through the actions, an evolution to mastery did not occur.

Decades later, I had an urge to see if I could still play the piano. I wanted to challenge myself with something outside of my normal routine. After becoming familiar with basic sheet music again, I quickly learned several songs and this time, I enjoyed it! In my first experience with the piano, my learning started with the actions. In the second experience, my learning started with a mindset. As you try the new approaches in this book, sometimes the action will feed the mindset and other times, the mindset will feed the action. I know that both approaches work, but it's been my experience that starting with an elevated mindset is more enjoyable and yields faster results.

WHERE ARE YOU?

If I'm headed out on a journey to a place I've never been before, the first thing I do is put the address into my GPS. What I don't see happening inside the GPS is that the first thing it does is locate where I am. It can't guide me to where I'm going without first knowing where I am. As a coach, I often observe entrepreneurs who are frustrated with where they are. Does this internal conversation sound familiar to you?

You're ready for a change. Maybe it's your industry, your niche, or your people, but your entrepreneurial brain is shouting at you, *Something has to change!* We're not talking about an overnight revolution, not an instant transformation, but an evolution that will stick. You've tried changing before, but you got tired and eventually, everyone went back to their old ways. Do you have the courage to try again?

Of course you do! It's what you do! This time is going to be different because we'll start with the core of all change: the way you're thinking about your thinking, or your mindset. It's not your people, your industry, your cash flow, or the weather that's hindering the evolution; it's you and the rules you've given your mind regarding the way to think.

Some leaders make the choice (sometimes unconsciously) to live in fear rather than courage. They put time and money into change tactics that never stick. They dabble in new initiatives and wonder why they aren't working. They constantly feel frustrated and out of control. Their people start to question the leadership asking, "Where are the changes you promised? Why aren't you doing what you say?" Fear rules in these companies; chaos rather than discipline controls management and decision-making. Lots of busy people are employed, but nothing is getting done. This is a recipe for entrepreneurial depression.

Once you adopt the Courage Mindsets, you'll see life differently. All decisions, discussions, and relationships will run through a new filter: your new way of thinking. With this new view on the world of your business, life won't be so messy. You'll calmly and confidently lead your company and your team to a fulfilled and profitable future.

Let's check in on where you are. Fill out this Courage Mindset Scorecard now, then fill it out again when you're done reading the book to see how much progress you've made. You can also access the scorecard online at http://bit. ly/couragescorecard.

So, are you ready to elevate your thinking and adopt the Courage Mindsets? If so, let's jump straight in!

Courage Mindset SCORECARD
for use with *The Courage Advantage* by Jill Young

STATEMENTS	1	2	3	4	5	6	7	8	9	10	11	12	Score	Goal
Discipline Your Time	You're too busy to stick to a schedule. Your daily to-do list is overwhelming. You have no time to give to people who need attention.			You plan to stick to a schedule but haven't figured out how yet. You've thought about hiring an assistant but don't have time.			You've mastered your time; others look to you as an example. You're proud of your discipline. Your assistant keeps your schedule straight.			You own your time. You've delegated so you can focus on your priorities. You have time to undertake new thinking, ideas, and the next big thing.				
Discipline Your Commitments	You commit to things you shouldn't only because you have no choice. You're paralyzed by your obligations.			One day, you can stop doing so much, but right now you're the only one who can do most things. Delegating tasks yields unpredictability.			You delegate most things you don't like but hold on to the important tasks because you need to be the final decision-maker.			You're careful with commitments and think about the benefits for the company. You have strong boundaries and focus on the company's needs.				
Discipline Your Thoughts	You can't keep up with everything you should think about for the future. You're in a cycle of worry and negativity about today's issues.			When you take the time to think, you have brilliant ideas, but distractions pull you away. You worry that others won't listen to your ideas.			You're well-read and know what's going on in the world. Other people respect your ability to apply the lessons you've learned.			You like input from trusted sources. You focus on short-term solutions and long-term vision. Thinking about your thinking is second nature.				
Lighten Up Your Reflections	It's ridiculous; the company keeps making mistakes. You make sure people know who's to blame. Your resentment toward others causes conflict.			Praising people is great, but you forget to do it. When you do, you notice the results. It's tiring keeping up with everyone and their work.			You plan fun activities, and everyone feels appreciated. People seem more comfortable being themselves, and that makes you feel optimistic.			When you slow down to celebrate wins and learn from losses in a fun way, it works. Your team's confidence skyrockets when they're recognized.				

xxii

Lighten Up Your Language	You're very serious in what you say. Being too casual causes people to lose their sense of urgency or causes authority to be minimized.	You'd like to have fun and laugh, but your problems are too serious. You're surprised when the fun people find satisfaction at work.	You hear laughter in the office. People like to work here; you're proud to be their leader. You make a point to seem like a real person.	You use laughter to keep the team going, which produces more creative, effective solutions. You're approachable and treat your team well.
Lighten Up Your Environment	You sometimes hear people complain about your office space. You like to keep costs down, so spending money on your office is low on your list.	You have ideas for creating a unique space but have a long way to go. Changing the work environment sounds great, but it makes you anxious.	Your offices are admired by others. You've spent money making sure people have what they need. Employees feel encouraged.	You create spaces that the team loves to be in and that communicate vision. You experiment with the environment, so people know you like new ideas.
Experiment with Curiosity	Your industry is late in the innovation game; there's not much to learn, but you worry competitors may have an advantage over your company.	You're sure you could do more for your customers if you only knew what it was. You worry that asking will make your company seem weak.	You ask customers if there's anything to improve. You create solutions they'll pay for. You feel there's more growth possible.	You always co-create solutions with your customers. They count on you to accelerate their growth. Your team tries new ideas and stays curious.
Experiment with a New Approach	What the company does now works well; your customers are satisfied. You can be pessimistic when others present new ideas.	You like new ideas, but they must produce results right away. You don't have time to mess up. You get irritated when new ideas don't work.	You're cutting-edge and have won awards for innovation in the marketplace. You've been recognized for your ideas and feel accomplished.	You love the phrase "Try it!" and engage the company in finding better ways to do what you do. Not every new approach works, and that's okay!
Experiment with Testing	Trying new things is a waste of effort and money. Even if you make some good progress, you like to stick with what works.	You try things but get frustrated if a client/team member isn't on board. You go back to old ways but are disappointed with the status quo.	You're at the top of your industry in customer satisfaction. You fix anything customers don't like so your reputation is not negatively affected.	Progress isn't easy, so you methodically iterate when you're experimenting. You don't get disappointed when your first try doesn't work.

The Courage to Have Discipline

Discipline shows up in leaders and teams in the form of good habits, in the way they think, and in the way they prepare for the day, events, and life in general.

The Courage to Lighten Up

Leaders can look at the world in a light, creative way rather than a serious, laborious way when they choose to celebrate small wins, reflect on the past to learn from it, and encourage possibility thinking.

The Courage to Experiment

Leaders who set up a culture of experimentation are open-minded, willing to try new ways of operating, and enter into new situations and conversations curious about the outcomes.

The Courage Mindset Model

This mindset model is designed to help you lead the evolution of your business faster and with less pain.

MINDSET 1
THE COURAGE TO
HAVE DISCIPLINE

This mindset requires a willingness to take control of your time, your commitments, and your thoughts. With this mindset, you'll be installing new, good habits, and uninstalling old habits that no longer serve you. You'll be committing to growing up and letting go of childhood rules of pleasing people. With the courage to be disciplined, you'll create habits that'll help you serve people and lead your company in doing the same. You'll reduce the chaos in your company and stop being the cause of it too!

BE DISCIPLINED WITH YOUR TIME

At some point, we learn that every human on the planet has the same time allotted to them: there are 24 hours in a day and 365 days in a year. So, how do some people seem to get more done in a day than others? They are disciplined with their time!

It starts with owning the fact that *you* are in charge of your time. Many leaders I begin to coach don't realize that they've created their own time monster because of their propensity to please other people. When we say *yes* to projects, patterns, or people that we aren't committed to, we've created a list of obligations of time that ends up turning our day into an unproductive mess.

Some leaders' confidence is even tied to others being dependent on their time. I call this the "busy badge," as if you get an award for being busy! (You don't.) Leaders who become disciplined with their time reclaim the privilege of owning the hours in their day. They start to see that being the only person who can do it is not contributing to the evolution of the business, and they begin to say *no* more often. They learn that being too busy really means they are too lazy to be disciplined with their time.

WAYS TO BE DISCIPLINED WITH YOUR TIME

Re-delegate to Your Direct Reports

As backward as it may seem, when you look at the to-dos on your plate, you might find that your direct reports have delegated tasks to you. Reverse this by making sure that you don't take over or finish projects for them, and don't rescue them by having tough conversations for them or make excuses for your team to other departments. Instead, engage in coaching them to find their own creative solutions.

If this is speaking loud and clear to you, but you're not sure how to reverse it, try this phrase: "Sarah, I've been rescuing you. There are several things (name them) that I've taken off your plate, and I need you to take them back. I'm still willing to coach you through the (things), but you'll be taking the action from now on."

Master Your Bookends

Most leaders have found that they have the most control over their time in the early mornings and the evenings, the bookends of their days. Take advantage of this and make it work for you. Have a solid morning and evening routine that allows space for you to think and rejuvenate.

Elements of these routines could include

- getting up before everyone else in your house
- meditating
- exercising
- getting sufficient sleep
- journaling
- updating your to-do lists
- reflecting on wins and goals for the day

Set Clear Meeting Rules

The Entrepreneurial Operating System's® Meeting Pulse Tool™ states that we should have meetings on the same day and at the same time each week. We should start and end every meeting on time and follow an agreed-to agenda.

Walter Krebs of Christmas by Krebs has a leadership team that is in four different time zones; part of the team is in Hong Kong. They found the right time to have their meetings, added video conferencing, and have had very productive meetings for five years! If they can do it, so can you.

Implement the Block-and-Tackle Method

Chunk your time in two-hour blocks for working on big projects, and other than physical breaks, don't do anything else during that time. Take breaks, but come back to the same project. In the book *Deep Work,* author and human optimization researcher Cal Newport states that tackling your mental, strategic, and important projects is best done two hours at a time—first thing in the morning and with no distractions.

Take Effective Breaks

Our brains can only stay effectively engaged for about 60-90 minutes before we need a five to 15-minute break. If you are working in blocks (the most effective way to work), then be sure you are taking effective breaks, too. Kristie Clayton, visionary of FIM (Female Integrator Mastermind), says that she has "started having dance breaks in the office when there is a celebration or a 'win.' It can be the tiniest of things, but the break feels so good!"

Tony Schwartz, founder of The Energy Project, teaches us why. His research shows that humans naturally move from full focus and energy to physiological fatigue every 90 minutes. Our body sends us signals to rest and renew, but we override them with coffee, energy drinks, and sugar. Or, we tap our reserves until they're depleted. Schwartz suggests that we need to purposely take short breaks every 90 minutes throughout the day to drink water, walk, or to eat healthy snacks.

One trick I use is called "do the opposite." If I'm working on a sedentary task, for my break, I'll get up and move. If I'm working inside, for my break, I'll go outside. If I'm working alone, for my break, I'll get social. If I'm working on the computer and my eyes are focused two feet in front of me, for my break, I'll look out to the horizon. During my sessions with clients, we often take breaks to do push-ups. Check out my research notes at the back of this book for why a push-up is the perfect exercise for breaks! (And you thought I was just a fitness nut!)

Avoid Decision Fatigue

Minimize the amount of time you allocate for making routine decisions by reducing your decision-making effort. Pre-decide everything you can. Here is a list of things I and other leaders pre-decide:

1. **What to wear:** I always wear the same type of pants, and all my shirts match all my pants, and then I pair them with the appropriate color of Chuck Taylors! I know a coach who bought five logo polo shirts and wore them for five straight years. I know a different leader who always wears a white shirt and black shoes. The only thing that changes is his pants, and since they never clash with black or white, he can literally grab a pair of pants in the dark and look good!

2. **What to have for breakfast:** I've been eating the same breakfast for 15 years! I never get bored with it because it's a non-event. It's been pre-decided! (If you are curious, it's basically a grilled cheese sandwich...LOL!)

3. **When to exercise:** It's not even a decision point for me in the morning. I just do it; it's built into my habits. The only bad workout is the one that doesn't happen.

4. **When to have planning meetings:** In the EOS Process®, the leadership team meets offsite, four times per year to work on the business. These all-day meetings happen no matter what daily event may distract the team. They never miss a session because it's been pre-decided, calendared, and committed to.

Proactive Teaching

Every hour you invest in teaching others the skills they need to get the job done will save you ten hours in the future. (Although this is a general claim, feel free to see my research notes at the back of this book.)

When you take time to teach others, it helps them feel, on a subconscious level, that they are valuable to you. This most often results in creative problem solving, higher productivity, fewer mistakes, less rework, and a lower overall turnover of the right people. Most of the time, entrepreneurs who operate in crisis mode are fighting the fires created by poorly-trained people in their organization. How much time could you save if everyone participated in high-quality training?

Jessica Staley of Datix created a library of videos that new and seasoned team members could use for training. Pretty soon, people in the company loved the library so much that everyone pitched in to create more videos.

Abe Canales of 3Sixty Integrated built a model of what a high-quality security closet looks like. The company uses the model to train new team members and do quality control inspections. This has allowed team members to give feedback to others on the job before there is a quality issue. When you take time to teach others, it helps them feel valuable. This will empower them to teach others.

Get an Assistant

In order for you and your company to evolve, you must focus your time on strategic tasks. You already know this, but I have coached leaders who are still doing 10-minute random tasks that add up to hours per week.

One visionary I worked with was late for a coaching call about an employee issue he was dealing with. Because he was late for the call, he felt like he needed to explain that he was late because he was buying water bottles for the shop and got stuck in the checkout line. More important than his original issue that day was getting an assistant to run errands like that for him.

As an Expert EOS Implementer®, I meet with my clients in full-day, in-person sessions in my session room in Dallas, Texas. Part of the preparation includes stocking water bottles and snacks, rearranging tables and chairs according to the size of the leadership team, and ensuring I have binders, books, markers, etc. This only took me 20 minutes each morning and 30 minutes each night. The time I spent in administrative tasks didn't feel significant until I added up that time over one year and found that it totaled 100 hours! When I hired my second assistant to take over the session room preparation, not only did I save myself 100 hours, but she significantly improved the layout, efficiency, and general awesomeness of the session room!

Eric Mattingly of Diversified Metroplex Investors was able to double the goals of his company once he got the right assistant in place. He found so much time in his daily schedule that he was able to dedicate more time to the big relationships he needed to develop to hit those goals.

Jenna Spencer, owner and visionary of AssistPro (a virtual assistant company that exclusively supports entrepreneurs and their leadership teams), reports that after just six weeks of being paired with the right assistant, 100% of her clients found more time in their day, more balance between their work and personal lives, and an overall decrease in stress.

Say "No" More Often

In the beginning of your career or this business, it was necessary for you to say *yes* a lot. It has gotten you this far. Courageous leaders start using the word no. No to the wrong opportunities, no to the longshots, no to the people or groups who are a time suck, no to the "shoulds" that other people place on you, no to opportunities outside your expertise.

Will Duke of 3Sixty Integrated recently stated, "Two years ago, if you would have told me that saying no to taking on additional work would increase our revenue and profit, I would have called you crazy. Now that we have a 15% swing upward in our bottom line, I call it smart!"

If you are still having a hard time saying no, channel your inner toddler; it's most likely the first word you learned! Sometime while growing up, we forgot how powerful it was!

BE DISCIPLINED WITH YOUR COMMITMENTS

When you do say yes, make it a *hell, yes!*

Leaders with courage say no a lot, but when they say yes, it's because it aligns with their stated goals and priorities. Once they've committed to something, they invest in it with both time and money. They follow through, asking for help and feedback along the way. Occasionally, when leaders fail to follow through with commitments, they are quick to own their results and tell their team and others early and honestly. These leaders know the benefits of being a good example to the whole company.

WAYS TO BE DISCIPLINED WITH YOUR COMMITMENTS

Who's up First?

Have a list of your standard priorities and filter your commitments through this list. For example, my "Who's up first?" list is:

1. Current clients

2. Graduated clients

3. Jill's sanity

4. Potential clients

5. Colleagues

6. Connectors

I give this list to my assistant, and she always knows where to prioritize my time. If my calendar is full of calls and meetings on a certain day and a client needs me, she knows to move a connector call to make room for the current client. This way, my clients always get to talk to me within 24 hours, even if I'm fully scheduled for the day.

Number three is in place because I will often take on too much if left to my own devices. Asking my assistant to get in the "Jill's sanity" game helps keep me disciplined. It's not easy to turn your life over to someone else, but the results are worth feeling the initial fear.

The One-Year Plan

Most companies create a plan for the year but then forget about it by March. Courageous leaders use the 1-Year Plan as a filter for what to say *hell, yes!* to. They say no to items that don't feed the success of the 1-Year Plan.

One of my favorite stories is about a 1-Year Plan that the team at LSR Commercial had committed to. They decided that this was the year to increase their ability to bid and dispatch work faster. The entire team went to work installing new software that would help them do this. They hired consultants, held training sessions, and then realized that the new software was actually holding them back from their goal of increasing their ability to bid and dispatch work quickly. They decided to treat the new software efforts as a sunk cost and went back to the old software, but with a new rigor to make it work. They kept trying new options until they were happy with their ability to bid and complete work. They stayed laser-focused on their goal and kept saying yes to getting to the finish line.

Memorize Your Lines

Create reusable sentences that you can use to get you through the emotional side of being disciplined with your commitments. Some phrases that I coach leaders to use are:

- When you are committed to being a great boss: "This is going to be a hard conversation." (When you need to have a commitment or recommitment conversation.) Or "I'm about to be very blunt." Or "We are not on the same page here; can we have a conversation?" Memorized lines can also be used when offering praise, such as "I'm throwing some appreciation your way." Or "That's exactly what (insert Core Value of the company here) looks like!"

- When you are committed to your previous priorities: "This is not the right time for me to commit to that." Or "If we do this, what will we not do? Is now the time to start that project?" and "Who can help you with this?"

Hard Now, Easy Later

Commit to the hard things first. Leaders with courage commit to tackling the hard things first. They've learned that if they do this, the little things fall into place or actually become easier to handle.

One leader had known for years that his CFO did not have the skills or stamina to take the company to the next level. Even though they had been friends since childhood, he let his CFO go, and both of them were relieved! Another leader had a hard conversation with his CFO, asking him to perform at a higher level. A few months later, when the CFO had failed to fulfill the request, the two of them had another honest conversation, and they decided that a different seat for him, still within the company, would serve everyone. Tip: People issues are always the hardest issues. Solve them first!

24 Hours

Give yourself 24 hours before saying yes. Ask yourself or your team, "Will this help us reach our goals? Is it the best thing that will help us reach our goals? What will we not do if we say yes to this? Could our time be better spent on a higher probability project/person/commitment?"

Keep in mind—the longer you take to get back to people with an answer of yes or no, the harder it is to say no. My dear friend John Pollock has been a champion of my work for years. Over the years of our friendship, he has recommended my work, bought my books, and attended my sessions. We've processed many personal and professional issues together, and I hold him in the highest regard. When he asked me to sit on his Board of Directors, I was both honored and crushed: honored that he would ask and crushed because I knew I had to say no. The time commitment just didn't align with my discretionary time. Although it was a tough conversation, we are still friends.

Have a List of Trusted People to Refer To

As much as I know I need to say no to some things, I still hate to tell people no, so I created a list of resources and am happy to point people and their requests in the right direction.

Recently, a client asked me to do sales training for their team. Although I *could* do the sales training, it would not help me reach my goals, and there was a much better expert I was able to direct them to. If you keep a list of trusted resources, you'll always have an answer to soften your real answer of no. It never feels like saying no when you can offer an alternative.

At the top of my list of resources are my "Five Best Friends." They are my best resources, people I rely on who will consistently respond and collaborate. For example, Michael Hall, Master Culture Index Consultant, is one of my best friends. When my clients struggle with getting the *right people* in the *right seats* according to The EOS® People Analyzer Tool™, I refer them to Michael and his tool that predicts human behavior in the workplace. I could certainly try to take on this task myself, but when Michael and I work together for the good of a client, magic occurs, and I stay true to my core commitments.

Have a One-System Rule

When keeping track of your commitments, keep track of them in one system. Some of you will choose good, old-fashioned notebooks, some will choose a calendaring system, and others will use the latest app, but don't use a mixture.

Courageous leaders experiment with several and stick with the one that works. Even if it can be embarrassing, as in my case. Since I was twelve, I have always used a pen-and-paper planner. These days, I use a three-subject spiral notebook with several pockets. (I get a new one each quarter.) Each section has a defined purpose, and I keep shorthand notes of all my clients on the inside of the back cover.

On a recent flight, I was flipping through it, making notes, and shuffling the stuff in the pockets when the man next to me commented, "A spiral notebook...are you 12?" Yes, thank you, I'm 12! I still love the colored pens and the ability to geek out with my notebook, especially when there is no Wi-Fi.

Leaders who become disciplined with their time find that they seem to have more of it. Creating space in your life for your most important activities benefits everyone you serve. Next, let's apply that discipline to your thinking.

BE DISCIPLINED WITH YOUR THOUGHTS

It matters what goes into your mind and when. Did you know that our brains are constantly scanning our environment for information? They are cataloging every input and thought, and it takes energy to do so. The brain uses what it needs and stores the rest or dumps it. For this reason, lots of leaders stay very conscious about what they allow into their brains and what they don't.

WAYS TO BE DISCIPLINED WITH YOUR THOUGHTS

Turn off the News

Decades ago, I decided to eliminate the news from my day. It started with needing more time to study for my master's program, but I soon realized the added benefit of not knowing what disaster, political argument, or scandal was happening in the world. And guess what? I loved it so much that I cut out all TV for a few years, only adding back programs that have purpose for me or people I serve.

How clear would your thoughts be if you created a space for silence where the news used to be? René Boer, co-author of *How to Be a Great Boss*, shared with me that he turned his news time into silence time on his drives into the office. He's disciplined and protective of that time and uses it to "focus on what the day will look like. I show up energized and prepared for a level-10 day!"

Only Check Your Phone on Purpose

Turning off notifications and checking your phone less often will help you stay focused and clear.

Recently, Cal Newport, one of my favorite researchers on optimizing our lives, published a book called *Digital Minimalism*. He teaches his readers to go on a digital fast and, when it's over, to only add back the apps that serve them.

Brian Johnson of Optimize.me teaches his followers to "Delete THAT app…you know which one, the one that wastes time for no benefit." For me, that app was Facebook. Sometimes, I found myself just scrolling mindlessly at the end of the day, using up precious time that I could have spent with my teenage sons.

Recently, a visionary I know deleted his email app from his phone. (That kind of courage even makes me sweat!) He reported that because of this, his entire leadership team started making better and faster decisions that moved the company forward. Be in charge of your phone; don't let it be in charge of you.

Surround Yourself with Other Courageous People

Find a group that encourages and nurtures your natural talents for leadership. Discontinue relationships or involvement with groups that engage in gossip, negativity, or defeatist thinking.

Strategic Coach, founded by Babs Smith and Dan Sullivan, is a group where I and my clients find this. Once a quarter, I gather with a group of people who *get* me. I formulate creative ideas with them. We motivate, challenge, and support each other. I often say it's like Disneyland for entrepreneurs!

One of my clients, Will Duke, recently told his team, "When I look back on my life, I'll divide it into two categories. One half is before Strategic Coach and the other half is after." Once he surrounded himself with courageous thinkers, his thinking reached a new level of courage and confidence as well.

Set Aside Time to Just Think

Put it on your calendar, and make a habit of sitting with your thoughts, plans, and dreams once a week. Keep a journal, using your own handwriting instead of typing your notes. Your brain thinks better that way. In EOS®, we call this a Clarity Break™.

This takes more courage than you think. Your thoughts are valuable to many people, and you may feel guilt for taking time away from others to focus on your thoughts. Keep this in mind: you *must* have clear thinking in order to give your people clear direction.

Stop Multitasking

Research has consistently found that multitasking results in more shallow thinking, less creativity, and a lower quality of work/product. Stephanie Long created "Rock time" at her company, ABGI. This is a two-hour block of time when everyone works on high priorities (called "rocks" after Stephen Covey's "first things first" principle in *The Seven Habits of Highly Effective Leaders* and a Foundational Tool in EOS®). This allows the phones to silence, the "hey, do you have a minute?" conversations to cease, and the barrage of intra-office emails to slow down while everyone is focused on their highest priority work.

REFLECTING ON THE COURAGE
TO BE DISCIPLINED

"I'm Not a Runner!"

In the fall of 2017, my friend, Annie, invited me to join her for a new type of workout that involved running. For my entire life, I had used the phrases "I'm not a runner" and "I despise cardio," but I indulged her and found that I actually liked most of the workout, except the running portion.

Six months into the nearly daily discipline of this new workout, I was still struggling with the running and kept using the phrase, *I'm not a runner,* yet, I was running about 10 miles a week. My coach challenged me by asking, "Is that what 'not a runner' looks like? If a person runs 10 miles a week, do you call that person a walker?"

I chose to evolve my mindset along with the internal narrative to "I'm a runner" and found that my behavior changed in a more effortless way. I started asking myself, *What would a runner do in this situation?* With my change in mindset, I made changes to my actions that felt effortless. I bought better shoes without second-guessing the investment. I drank more water without "shoulding" myself and woke up with less grogginess because *that's what a runner does.*

Do you already have disciplined habits that you are discounting? Are you telling yourself a story about discipline that doesn't serve you? Where in your life are you *not a runner?*

Time to Think About Your Thinking!

In this coaching guide for reflection, I encourage you to take as much time in reflection as you did to take in the information. Reflection is the new, fourth R in learning (Reading, wRiting, aRithmetic, and Reflection).

Reflection helps the concepts sink in and helps you avoid the common response—those are good ideas—but never applying them. So, even if it's a small change (small changes are the basis of the evolution model after all), reflect on *something* you will do this week in order to apply what you've learned. I've provided a coaching guide here with space here for you to write, but feel free to use your own reflection ideas as well.

1. Let's get this reflection started with thinking about ways you are already displaying the courage to be disciplined. List them here:

   a. With my time:

   _____

   _____

   b. With my thoughts:

   _____

   _____

   c. With my commitments:

   _____

   _____

2. In this chapter, there were more than 20 ideas and examples of how leaders like you choose to have the courage to be disciplined. What concepts resonated with you? What could you do to be more disciplined?

_____

_____

3. From those ideas, list the actions that you will take this week.

_____

_____

4. What might get in your way of doing those things this week?

_____

_____

5. How will you overcome those obstacles?

_____

_____

6. Based on your answers to the above questions, is there anything you could do next quarter or next year? Write it here so you can come back to it. There are no unrealistic goals, only unrealistic time frames.

_____

_____

MINDSET 2
THE COURAGE
TO LIGHTEN UP

Have you ever noticed that popular teachers, speakers, and trainers often start their learning sessions with a joke or some funny observation? Conversely, do you remember sitting in school or a conference when the teacher started the lesson by reading the syllabus or going over the rules of what not to do?

The first type of teacher knows that having a light-hearted approach to learning and communicating helps the concepts stick. They know that engaging the audience or students with laughter infuses their subconscious with thoughts like, *I'm going to like this! This is enjoyable! This is a good use of my time! I like this person!*

You certainly could drive your way to change like the second kind of teacher, with muscle, grit, and hard fights. While grit certainly has a place in discipline, I've found that teams and leaders who evolve faster and with less stress decide to have some fun along the way. Just as our bodies need rest and work cycles, so do our brains. Adding fun, laughter, and lightheartedness to your approach supports this natural cycle.

As David Rock explains in his SCARF model from the article "Managing with the Brain in Mind," when a person is feeling lighthearted and creative, the chemical oxytocin is flowing throughout their body. Oxytocin supports a feeling of "Let's go, we can do this!"—essentially a positive outlook on life and all the possibilities there are in the world.

When people are stressed or feeling fearful, the chemical cortisol is more prevalent. Cortisol not only wreaks havoc on the body, it also puts our brain in survival mode (think fight or flight), where we literally (yes, I used the word *literally*) cannot think or learn, only react.

If you are pushing for change with sheer will, threats, or force, you are perpetuating the resistance to change. How would it affect the motivation in your company if you had the courage to embrace this lighter approach, especially when things aren't going as planned? Creating an enthusiastic, light-hearted culture might just accelerate the change, help it feel like an evolution, and help it stick.

LIGHTEN UP YOUR REFLECTIONS

Reflecting on a project, goal, or desired outcome after the fact is a proactive practice that some companies fail to implement. Reflection gives the brain a chance to let both positive and negative learning sink in. Taking a positive approach to these reflections is something courageous leaders make time for.

When failures occur, courageous leaders lead with learning. Upon reflecting on the event, they take a "What did we learn?" approach, inviting people to reflect on the less-than-desirable outcome. Leaders who take the blame-and-shame approach won't get the best out of their people. The cortisol produced during the rant will prevent the people involved from engaging in a higher order of thinking about what to change the next time around.

Additionally, courageous leaders know that reflecting on and focusing on the positive outcomes (even if they are small) more than the negative outcomes produces more positive results. They calendar and prioritize praising people and projects often.

WAYS TO LIGHTEN UP YOUR REFLECTIONS

Hold a Lessons Learned Session

Before diving into *What went wrong?*, start with *What went right?* Oftentimes, we don't know where the project went off the rails because we can't isolate the working parts from the non-working parts.

This year, Kevin Lackey of Freedom Powersports asked his leadership team to take a one-hour Clarity Break™ to reflect on the greatness—personal and professional—of the year. Then, he asked them to dream about the possibilities for next year. In the past, he would ask things like, "Why were your numbers off this year, and what will you do to make sure your numbers are on for next year?" While diving into the numbers certainly has its place, this year's new approach produced much more creative, open, and honest reflections, and dreams.

You can even do a personal "Lessons Learned" variation on a daily basis. During the course of the day, there are likely several things that you fixed or several things that went wrong. Ending your day by journaling or simply highlighting to yourself three things that you learned goes a long way to getting your brain to focus on the positive.

Find Ways to Celebrate on Regular Basis

Some of my clients have created light-hearted awards with fun names. They make sure there is very little bureaucracy in the way of team members obtaining these awards, and they don't engage in a "well, she won last time, so we can't give it to her" approach. They favor recognizing people often instead of just once a year or once a quarter. They've also found that casual, peer-to-peer recognition is an accelerator for evolution.

Thomas Holland of Apex Surface Care and Corporate Floors created clever awards such as "The Firefighter," "The Big Dog," "The Elephant," "The Ultimate Fighter," and "The Helping Hand." You don't even need to know what these awards represent to know that it would be fun to work in this company! During one particularly busy quarter, Thomas even made sure that spontaneous celebrations were high priorities by making them *rocks*!

In the company that I previously led, we had a "traveling rock star." It was a simple, shiny, cardboard star that was passed around from person to person whenever we saw someone making a rock star move for the company or a client.

Ash Wineinger and his team at Capital Precast made Core Value stickers that they hand out spontaneously when someone is observed following the Core Values. Big and little examples count. The team members there have started placing the stickers on their hard hats to show healthy pride in their contribution to a safe and healthy culture. Conversely, one day when Ash walked onto the shop floor without a hard hat, one of the supervisors handed him a written warning. Everyone smiled and had a hearty laugh at the boss's error, but they also celebrated because they have a culture of safety first, and no one, including the owner of the business, is exempt from the rules.

Use the "How Can We...?" Brainstorming Method

When teams feel in a rut, like there is nothing to be done, ask them to engage in a brainstorming game called "How can we...?" Write the phrase on the board and ask them to come up with possibilities. For fun, you can ask the team to *oooh* and *ahhh* after each suggestion; remember, in brainstorming, there are no bad answers!

Mike Ivey of Modern Message was concerned that the company wouldn't be able to hire fast enough to fulfill customer needs. When we processed the issue leading with "How can we...?", after about 15 minutes, we had our priority hires agreed to and action steps defined and committed to.

Try the "What Would Be a Fun Way to...?" Brainstorming Method

The format is similar to the "How can we...?" method, but this one adds an extra element of fun. Keep in mind that both of these exercises are not meant to find the right answer, but to get the creative juices flowing so that teams *can* find the right answer.

The leaders at EzBel Construction knew they wanted to honor a retiring city employee, but with only two weeks before his departure, they felt limited with their obvious choices. When we approached the issue with "What would be a fun way to do this?", they came up with the idea to invite him to the company family Christmas party that was only days away. What better way to honor a civil servant than to have them surrounded by their constituents and their families? They took pictures and created a thank-you poster from the team for him to keep. It was a powerful moment for all involved.

Just Add Music

Anytime you need a message or reflection to really stick, just add music! John Bentley of RAA composed a rap of the company's Core Values, and although some might tease him that it wasn't really musical, per se, it definitely lifted spirits and created a solid memory.

Brad Casebier of Radiant Plumbing uses music as a rule in all of his meetings. He even has theme songs for different people on his team. He's mastered the art of using the volume to bring people back to attention and to get them to converse.

Attending his meetings is a such a treat that Michelle Heater, the recruiter for Radiant Plumbing, insists that all qualified applicants get a chance to be in one of the meetings. She reports that this is where they decide they would love to work for Radiant.

John Hinckley of Modern Message asked his leadership team to star in five music videos, one for each Core Value of the company. Imagine seeing these videos during a job interview or on a website. Immediately, you know these are courageous, creative believers in their company and passion!

LIGHTEN UP YOUR LANGUAGE

Courageous leaders have learned the power of being real and simple. They drop their egos and any social masks they are wearing. They stop protecting themselves and their image, and they start to engage as humans.

Most often, I've noticed that the first place for this to appear is in how they talk to each other. These leaders drop the flowery, academic language, and simply say what needs to be said. They stop using acronyms and long stories to get their point across and simply state their point. They stop taking themselves and their team members so seriously.

Occasionally, because I have a "you can say anything in this room" rule when we are in session, the leaders curse, cry, yell, hug, throw things, collapse into the bean bag, spin on their chairs, tease each other (and me!), and engage in general silliness—like real humans do. The fact is, the more courageously human the leaders become, the bigger impact they have on the evolution of the company.

WAYS TO LIGHTEN UP YOUR LANGUAGE

The Name Game

Invent creative names for mundane or complex things that would ordinarily have very long or boring names. For example, Jacob Midel from Regal Plastics came up with a method whereby the sales people would have some flexibility on the price that they quoted their customer based on prior bids, the going profit margin, and several other factors. When he referred to this concept, he called it the Bob Barker. So, even though the concept was complex, he simplified it by giving it a simple name that everyone used when referring to the approach.

When my team agreed to our processes, we gave them fun names involving theater terms. When we start a new client, we have a *Rehearsal* process. After every session, I follow the *Show Notes* process. Even our titles are fun! We could have given Stephanie the title of Supplies and Inventory Coordinator, but that would have been boring. Her title is *Stage Manager!*

The team at Think Why, led by their Integrator Claudine Zachara, has agreed to some fun terms and has even created a slide deck describing them as part of their onboarding process. When the team is making a decision and wants to make sure everyone is committed, they call it *stacking hands*. When it's time to end a meeting, celebrate, or shout out some praise, they yell, "10!" (Of course, you'll need to work there before they tell you the secret behind why they do that!)

When a techy person is about to explain techy stuff to non-techy people, they have permission to replace the technical jargon with the words "clackity clack." Everyone in the company knows this language and uses it. Not only is this approach light-hearted, but it also reduces confusion. Too many times, I've helped clients solve issues only to realize that there was no issue; they were talking about the same thing but using different words.

The Secret Hashtag

Create a hashtag for some important goal or initiative you want to create energy around. For example, one of my clients has a moonshot goal to have 10 locations by 2025, so they created the hashtag #big1025. They use this for their Wi-Fi passwords, put it on email signatures, and have it built into subtle places on their website. No one outside the company knows what it means, but when the employees reflect on it, it reminds them, in a fun way, of the big goal.

Toys for Talking With

Meetings are one of the places where we can communicate in a fun, real way. Try adding some toys that help people stay on track or say what they need to say in a light-hearted way. You can use the stress ball style suggestions below or make up your own.

1. Horse—To say, "You're beating a dead horse."

2. Cow—We might be in "sacred cow" territory.

3. Squirrel—We are going off on a tangent.

4. Pig—We might not be looking at reality (when pigs fly).

5. Donkey—Someone is being an *ass!*

6. Monkey—Someone is trying to pass off their monkey (their problem).

Share Your Personal Histories

This easy exercise has done more to bond teams that I work with than any other. It originated in the book *The Five Dysfunctions of a Team*, by Patrick Lencioni, and was adapted by Gino Wickman for use by companies running on EOS®. Ask everyone to share the following with the group (and you get to go first!):

1. Where did you grow up?

2. Tell us about the number of siblings you have and where you are in that birth order.

3. What was your greatest challenge growing up?

4. Tell us about your first job.

5. Tell us about your worst job.

6. Share something unique that no one here knows about you.

Once, while doing this exercise as part of an EOS® Annual Planning Session, a client of mine had two people on the leadership team who were at constant odds with each other. When the team engaged in this simple exercise, they realized that they both shared a childhood trauma—both of their sisters had died as a result of leukemia. After hugging it out on the break, the tension between them instantly disappeared and although there was still healthy ideological debate, their personal issues melted away once they saw each other as humans with real human stories.

Build In Laughter

Make laughter a part of the routine! One of the objectives of all of my more than 500 sessions has been to have fun. I build jokes (even lame ones), push-up contests, victory laps, high fives, and sometimes even skipping (if you earn it) into every session because it creates the space for creative problem solving to occur. And well, I like to laugh, too!

Rod Coleman of SYM Financial tells a cheesy joke just before he starts every meeting. Brandon Barr of Regal Plastics invites people who have exceeded their monthly goals to shoot hoops to earn extra bonuses. The whole division gathers to cheer them on. Ron Pyke, my fractional CFO, has a bicycle horn in his office. His colleagues are encouraged to "toot their own horn." Every week as they gather for meetings, they share good news from their week with a toot. I smile just writing about it!

Be Generous and Creative with Your Appreciation

While everyone likes to be appreciated, not everyone likes to be appreciated in the same way. Apply the Platinum Rule to appreciation. The Golden Rule is to treat others as you'd like to be treated. The Platinum Rule is to treat others the way they would like to be treated. Extroverts like public praise. Introverts like something more private.

To truly appreciate someone, consider starting with active listening. Do you know what's going on in their life? What are their interests? Once you have the answers, create appreciative experiences for them that align with where they are in life.

Imagine the surprise a brand-new employee felt when the leadership team showed up at her house to help her move to a new apartment that was closer to the office. The team's creative approach was much more valuable than a welcome basket.

LIGHTEN UP YOUR ENVIRONMENT

Unlike regular, static companies, an evolving company thrives best in an environment that breathes and grows with it. Courageous leaders know that people are a product of their environment. They will reflect the energy and spirit of the four walls that they occupy.

WAYS TO LIGHTEN UP YOUR ENVIRONMENT

Go Visual

Virtually all of my clients have discovered the benefit of prominently displaying their core values as a reminder to everyone inside and outside the company who they are at their core.

Don Janacek of FreshOne created the "Wallsome" in his office. "A giant wall of awesome," he calls it. On the wall, he displays the company's core values along with the faces of the people who are currently being recognized for exemplifying them.

Christine Magrann, from Makeready, has added the company's guiding principles into their new hire on-boarding and leadership development sessions, included them in birthday cards and daily staff line-ups, and painted them prominently in team member hallways.

Many leadership teams have created recognition programs for team members who display these values in a meaningful and impactful way. I've also seen motivating and uplifting declarations of unity and purpose displayed as plaques, written on simple poster board, or stenciled on windows.

Go Physical

Brad and Sarah Casebier of Radiant Plumbing took the environment to a whole new level when they set a goal to buy a boat for their employees to use, which also turned into a pretty cool commercial about surfing on a toilet. Their next goal is to install a go-kart track! They also kick off all of their meetings with a quick dance session to outrageous music. They'll take breaks to learn how to "floss" or engage everyone with a game of dodgeball.

Get Creative and Collaborative

Heather Ettinger of Luma Wealth Advisors put a 1000-piece puzzle in a common space where team members would walk by it throughout the day. Employees would stop and place a few pieces while getting to know other people from outside of their department.

Katrina Keys of K Strategies has a glass container on a table in the common room labeled "K Strategies' Rocks." Every time someone completes a Rock (a 90-day, high-priority task), they put a real rock in the glass container. Everyone gets to see the company's progress.

At EZBel, Stephen Park posts the Rock Sheets of any department that obtains 100% completion on the conference room wall. He plans on keeping them there forever, for history's sake.

REFLECTING ON THE COURAGE TO LIGHTEN UP

"I'm the Boss! You Can't Talk to Me That Way!"

The courage in lightening up comes when you, yes, *you,* share your humanity with the people you are leading, especially when you make mistakes. It takes courage to live by the vision you have sold the company.

Chad Gono of Regal Plastics tells a story of a time when the leadership team was placing a particular emphasis on living by the core values that are on our wall. After a heated meeting with some salespeople, a fairly new employee singled Chad out for not leading with positivity (one of their core values). Chad recalls that, "I really wanted to say, 'I'm the boss; you can't talk to me that way!' But instead, I realized that this was exactly what we'd been working for: an environment where everyone is open and honest and feels comfortable giving feedback."

Chad points to that moment as the point when he realized what it felt like to choose the company's best interests over his ego. It was a big moment of courage for him and his company. They stepped back into the issue with a positive focus, laughed about the irony, and got back to work with grateful hearts.

Having the courage to lighten up pays in dividends of an engaged company full of team members who are ready and excited to be creative, engage in deep, possibility-based thinking, and work more productively. How far could you go if you chose to *lighten up?*

Time to Think About Your Thinking!

Yes, let's reflect again. This time, we'll reflect on how you can have the courage to *lighten up*.

1. Let's start with celebrating how you are already showing the courage to lighten up. What is already working for you? List those things here:

   a. With my reflections:

   _____

   _____

   b. With my language:

   _____

   _____

   c. With my environment:

   _____

   _____

2. In this chapter, there were more than 20 ideas and examples of how leaders like you chose to have the courage to lighten up. What concepts resonated with you? What could you do to be more lighthearted?

   _____

   _____

3. From those ideas, list the actions that you will take this week.

   _____

   _____

4. What might get in your way of doing those things this week?

_____

_____

5. How will you overcome those obstacles?

_____

_____

6. Based on your answers to the above questions, is there anything you could do next quarter or next year? Write it here so you can come back to it. There are no unrealistic goals, only unrealistic time frames.

_____

_____

MINDSET 3
THE COURAGE
TO EXPERIMENT

The courage to experiment is based on the principle of hope. I don't mean the wishful thinking type of hope found in fairy tales, but the hope I'm referring to is the deep knowledge that there is always a solution, we just have not found it yet.

Entrepreneurs who lead the evolution of their companies are constantly experimenting with ways to make things better. For some team members, the leader may seem like she is unfocused or constantly changing her mind, but at her core, she's a scientist, forming a hypothesis and ready to test it with an experiment.

We never lose when we embark on an experiment. We either win, or we learn valuable insights for the next experiment. This experimentation mindset requires the understanding that you do not need to be sure of the outcome in order to try something new. And stepping into the unknown takes lots of courage!

EXPERIMENT WITH CURIOSITY

Leaders who get curious on purpose have the courage to ask others what they think. Initiating a conversation with a team member about what they think is working or not working only yields results when they can sense that you really want to know. Asking clients for feedback in a curious way involves another level of curiosity, a humble curiosity.

You need to be humble enough to know that there is feedback to be heard. Listening to the answers to the questions you are curious about takes discernment and a thin skin, not a tough one. Tough skins don't let the critical information in. Having the courage to be curious means you are inviting others to examine even the dark corners of the closets you might not want to open. It means that you are inviting people to bring up new issues, and you get to be fearless in being willing to help sort them and solve them.

WAYS TO EXPERIMENT WITH CURIOSITY

Build a Team

You cannot live on Curiosity Island on your own because you already know what you know. Build a team that is excited to get all issues solved. Make sure this team is made up of individuals who share your Courage Mindset and who are capable of organized, productive thinking. Having a strong team will reduce the fear it takes to get really curious.

Keyan Zandy of Skiles Group so passionately believes in curiosity that he advocated for it as a Core Value of the company. With curiosity at the heart of the team, Skiles Group has been able to prevent issues and create new ways of operating outside of industry norms. Being open to different ways of thinking and getting curious about others' ideas is often what helps a team get unstuck from a previously unsolvable issue.

Ask Great Questions, and Keep Asking Them

Here are a few of my favorite questions that get the most honest answers:

1. *What's on your mind?* This question and the one following were introduced to me in the book *The Coaching Habit* by Michael Bungay-Stanier. Use this question when someone says, "Do you have a

minute?" or, "Can we chat?" For good reasons (that Michael explains in his book), this response cuts out the chit chat and is more effective at getting right to work on the issue.

2. *What else?* A follow-up to *What's on your mind?* or any other open-ended question, this is a strategy many coaches use because we've discovered that the first part of the exchange is rarely the heart of the issue. When you ask, "What else?" the brain digs deeper, often getting closer to the real issue.

3. *Can you walk me through your thought process?* Use this question when you'd rather say "What the f*%$ happened?!?" or when you perceive that a mistake has occurred. The reason this question is so effective is that it does not place judgment on the person being questioned. When people feel judged, they instinctively want to defend themselves. Asking the question this way is a truly curious way for you to get to the heart of the issue and for the person to find their own mistake, which helps the lesson stick!

4. *What do you need (to make that happen, to be successful, to take the next step, etc.)?* Use this question when it feels like there are a lot of excuses or blaming going on. This question cuts past the past and sends the team member's brain to the future. The past is the past; let's move on and get to a solution. This is also a good question to use when someone is trying to pass the accountability on to someone else. Saying, "What do *you* need?" implies that you need them to take ownership and lead toward the solution.

5. *What does done look like?* This question invites the person to look further into the future. It asks them to really visualize the final product. It also helps them

to tie the project or concern to the purpose. This can also help people naturally create mini-milestones for themselves because they start with the end in mind and work backward through the milestones they must hit in order to be done by a certain date.

Be Switzerland

Leaders who are not *truly* curious cast judgment (either positive or negative) on the answers from team members and thereby taint the experiment of curiosity. Instead of showing extreme positive or negative emotion when someone comes to you with an issue (something that stayed hidden from you until you got curious,), show interest instead. You can even use the words, "That's interesting; tell me more." Not taking sides on the issue right away will encourage your people to continue being open and honest with you.

One of the leaders I coached was getting frustrated with the fact that his team was not being open and honest with him about their ideas or concerns. He asked me to coach him on how to get this to happen. As I observed him in our next session, I noticed that when he asked a question and someone on his team would start to answer, he responded by shaking his head up and down if he agreed or side to side if he didn't agree. Essentially, his body language was leading the team to say only what they thought he approved of them saying. He humorously called his behavior "bobble heading" and has since corrected it to get better collaboration.

Deal with "I Don't Know" Responses

Sometimes, when leaders start to get curious, they are met with an answer of "I don't know." Fortunately, you don't have to live with that answer! Take the time to dig deeper.

It's been my experience that when someone says "I don't know," it usually means "I haven't had time to think about it" or "I'm not interested in thinking about it." 80 percent of the time, if you give someone two quiet minutes to think about it, something will appear.

Another tool is to say, "You don't have to *know*. I'd just like to hear your ideas about what it *could* be." If you feel someone is truly not interested in thinking about it, you can use the phrase, "I'd like you to come up with some ideas. Where will you start looking? Who else could you talk to that might know?" We want to get their brain cells moving!

Use the Angel's Advocate Approach

Use this approach when a new idea has been proposed that is met with initial resistance. First, establish that the devil's advocate will have his due...in due time. But first, we will listen to the angel's advocate. For two minutes, we'll only talk about how and why this idea would work.

The reason this tool works is that it's easy for the brain to find problems with a new approach. It is harder for the brain to see why it will work. This is also a great tool that fosters listening, possibility thinking, and creativity.

EXPERIMENT WITH A NEW APPROACH

Courageous leaders don't just know that *what got you here won't get you there.* They actively seek new approaches; they try new things to get them to a new place. For these leaders, there are no sacred cows; they are open to trying new approaches in every facet of their business. They know that they'll need to try lots of different things in order to find the things that work. They are willing to keep trying until they nail it. For these leaders, failure only gets them closer to success. They are willing to invest with time and money.

WAYS TO EXPERIMENT WITH A NEW APPROACH

The Third Time's the Charm

This simple concept is based on Dan Sullivan's *The 80% Approach*™. Once you decide to try something new, give it three good chances to work. When we do anything the first time, the most correct we'll ever get is 80%. Try the same thing again, and chances are you'll be 96% right. Try it a third time, and you may be 99.2% right. If it's still not what you are looking for after three tries, *then* consider trying something else, but don't throw the idea out on the first try.

When I'm coaching companies how to run on The Entrepreneurial Operating System® (EOS®), I set the expectation that implementing the system is typically a two-year process. I teach the tools to the leadership team in a certain sequence, and then the leadership team teaches their direct reports, who teach their direct reports. Most teams take about three tries (or three quarters) to master the basic tools; they give their direct reports the same grace.

If you have perfectionists on your team, use them wisely. Get them involved with the project on the third try, not the first or second. Asking perfectionists to kick off a project often results in delays getting started because they want it to be perfect from the beginning, which is unrealistic. Use their eye for excellence once the big bugs have worked out. They can make the third time really shine!

Imagine Life without Your Sacred Cow

The term "sacred cow" refers to any idea, custom, or situation that is above criticism or above questioning. (Examples of sacred cows include: the actions or responsibilities of the owner; a large, profitable customer; or a piece of proprietary software.) If you have a sacred cow, ask your team to imagine life without it. For example, "What if Bill couldn't call all the clients back within 24 hours?" or "What if we didn't serve ABC company as our largest client?" If you honestly talk through the scenarios as if the sacred cow was absent, you might just realize that life would not end if we killed the sacred cow.

Blue Label Farms received 25% of their income from a large customer that they were serving in a very custom way. For years, the sentiment in the company was to take care of this customer at all costs because of the cash flow contribution. When they examined life without this sacred customer, they discovered that the customer was not profitable, caused internal strife and stress, and required the company to keep investing in capital that would not pay off in the long run. It took lots of courage and a willingness to go backwards in revenue, but when they let the customer go, profits, morale, and focus improved.

Another example of killing a sacred cow comes from a father and son team in the manufacturing business. For decades, the son (and the company) knew that he was being groomed to take over the family business. Through a series of conversations and confrontation, we asked the question "What if he doesn't?" When we isolated the emotion and took it out of the equation, the outcome would actually be better for the father and the son if the son did *not* to take over the business.

What is curious about this situation is that after the emotions were back in line, and we added some discipline and accountability to both the father and the son's behaviors, the son decided in a very healthy, non-sacred way, that he *did* want to participate in the business, just in a different role.

See the Little Things

Try making simple and small moves. Sometimes leaders fall in love with their big ideas when, in reality, a small change can produce powerful results.

For Tyler Guidry and Ben McCraw of Accomplice, innovation *is* their business. In their podcast, "It's Worth Doing Right," they say that one of the ways they help their clients create immersive marketing experiences is by analyzing the little things that are missing or that could enhance the experience. It's generally the little changes rather than the big changes that transform a product into an experience.

Tom Ackerman of SYM Financial tells the story of a process that the team had outgrown. An idea surfaced from two of the team members around a small change and it worked. He also mused that had the leadership team tried to fix this, they might have come up with a more drastic change when all that was needed was a tweak. Getting the right people on the solution works.

Jeff Griffiths of Miller and Associates was anticipating that major changes needed to happen within the structure of his company. As he was contemplating the options, one of his team members made the comment, "It would be easier if I were just on Greg's team. That way, we'd all be on the same page." His comment gave Jeff the idea to organize the company into divisions instead of territories, and the team was on board. There were no promotions, demotions, firings, or hirings of new people needed, just a simple realignment of how they were communicating.

Take a Longer Perspective

You know your clients are changing and growing and you love that. This means that they'll always need more from you. One way to stay ahead of their needs is to get your people thinking into the future. Ask questions of your team like "What will our customer need next year? What do they wish we did that we don't do yet?" Even better still, ask your customers these questions.

Walter Krebs of Christmas by Krebs is in an industry with traditionally long sales cycles. When they posed these questions to their team and their customers, they became aware of the need to mentally become a weekly company rather than the traditional seasonal company. They needed to shorten production times, have the ability to customize ornaments instantly, keep up with and predict trends, etc. As a result of this thinking, they have systematically changed their customer and product mix.

When the Blankinship and Foster team decided to upgrade their operating software, they chose to install an industry-leading product. While in the implementation period, they found that several areas of the software were lacking in functionality. Rather than getting upset and moving to another product, they took a long-term approach and chose to contribute time and energy to coaching the software vendor, using the power of cooperation to build something great for an entire industry.

Employ the Blank Slate Method

Sometimes, the thing holding us back from a new approach is everything that is on our list today. Ask the team to imagine that this is a brand-new company, and we need to be ready to handle our current volume of customers tomorrow. *How would you do it? What seats do we need? What do our processes look like?* Keep in mind that as you try this approach with your team, you'll need to keep reminding them that this is a blank slate day!

When the team at Grating Systems took this approach to their bonus structure, they found several things they wanted to change. Over a period of two years, they systematically restructured their incentive plan by committing to moving away from what just felt good, to what the company needed to succeed, and for everyone to feel "grate."

EXPERIMENT WITH TESTING

Imagine a building with many foyers, hallways, and connecting doors. Somewhere in that building, behind one of those doors, is a treasure. You have no map; the only way to find it is to explore the building. You won't know what you'll find until you go in the first door. When you enter the first door, there are three more doors. But you didn't know that until you entered the first door.

Entrepreneurs call this concept The Adjacent Possible (borrowed from a concept by Stuart Kauffman, a theoretical biologist). This is where one choice leads to the next set of options, but you don't know what those options are until you take action or *test* the first choice.

Until you have the courage to take action and *do* something, your thinking just stays in your brain; it ends up as just a wish or a theory. Scientists know that sudden, big breakthroughs are rare, but what they count on is all the small learning, tweaks and trials that test minor variables one at a time. All of this coalesces into a solution that can be award-winning.

Leaders with a Courage Mindset also understand that small and simple things (tests) bring about greater things. I've also observed that these leaders take action, even if it's a small action. They consistently take small steps toward the big goal, even if the initial step isn't in the direction they want to go.

WAYS TO EXPERIMENT WITH TESTING

Use the Word *Experiment*

When you are ready to try something new and you need to get people to buy into it, use the word *experiment*. It makes the change feel less final and concrete. For example, "We are going to experiment with a new schedule: We are going to open at 8:00 a.m. instead of 9:00 a.m. to see how it helps our foot traffic," instead of, "We will now be opening the store at 8:00 a.m. to increase the amount of foot traffic." We don't *know* that opening the store early will help the issue; we are going to test it out to see if it will help.

A lot of people are fearful of change because it feels final. When in reality, nothing is ever final. (Okay...death and taxes. ☺) When Justin Harlin and Matt Wilkeson of Smile Fort Worth decided they wanted to expand their dental practice, they were pretty sure that they'd need a killer marketing department. When the rest of the team was hesitant, they asked if they could just have their commitment to try it, not commit to it forever.

When Chris Goade of 360 Consulting knew he had to change the sales meeting structure with a very seasoned sales team, he proposed a new structure as an experiment. The team committed to adhering to the new structure for three months. After the three months, they all felt it was valuable enough to keep going. Most people are willing to try if they know that it might not be a forever thing. Of course, when it works, there is proof instead of conjecture, and people love what works.

Test It on the Right People

Strategic Coach calls this method "Test it with check writers." When you are trying something new for a customer, before you finalize the project and print the literature, test it out with a few (or more) customers. Current customers make great test subjects.

When I had the idea for my Mastermind Advantage series, I sent out an email to my top clients describing what it was, how I planned to run it, and asked them if they would consider buying in. When I got 20 yeses in three days, I knew I had created something valuable.

A year earlier, I did the same thing with a Coaching School for Managers that I had created. That idea was met with a wet blanket response, so I revised it until it turned into the Accountability Activator Workshop, which is now consistently sold out. Had I put efforts into building out the coaching school without testing it with my check writers, I would have been very frustrated.

When Will Duke of 3Sixty Integrated had an idea that would take care of his customers' full life cycle of security, he put it in front of his biggest customers first. To his surprise, one feature of his idea was extremely exciting to them, whereas the rest of it received a less enthusiastic response. Because of this information, he was able to train his salespeople to lead with the popular feature and adjust the roadmap so that the feature was made a priority. This was all because he tested his idea with his biggest check writers. The wrong people to test it on are your spouse, your buddies, or even your colleagues. Test it on whomever will benefit from the change.

Delegate in Chunks

In an ever-evolving company, delegating the right tasks to the right people is an everyday practice. Additionally, positions are being created and there are seats to be filled on a regular basis. In order to make sure your people are ready for promotions and to create expanded capabilities in your company, make it a habit to delegate parts of your job to your people before you need to. It takes someone courageous to train someone to take over their job in a proactive way. If something doesn't go well, or someone is not capable of the task, you'll know it by testing it out rather than just assuming that they'll be able to do it one day.

John Bentley of RAA had a talented young accountant whom he wanted to be the company's CFO one day. Instead of waiting until he was ready for the CFO role, he started Josh on certain CFO tasks right away. As the quarters went by, he delegated more and more to Josh. When Josh was moved to the CFO seat, he was fully prepared and experienced very little pain in the transition. By not expecting perfection from day one, John and Josh were able to test and iterate the job functions little by little.

Get the MVP in Place

Nope, not the most valuable player—the Minimally Viable Product. This is the concept of getting the most basic product (or process, location, person, etc.) in place right away rather than waiting until the product is complete before releasing it. This is a must for some industries (technology) but other industries can follow their lead.

When George Baker of ParkHub brought on several stadiums at once, the team had to install the MVP right away and systematically add the upgrades as the months went by.

Had they waited until the product was 100% complete, they would have missed several profitable seasons.

When David Oles of AgVantis promised his customers a full cybersecurity package, they installed the minimum right away, and over the course of 18 months will add all the bells and whistles.

Watch the Eyebrows

Eyebrows can't lie. When explaining a thought, process, or new concept to people, watch for their eyebrows to lift. When they do, they are with you; this means they like what they are hearing.

Most of us have been raised to be agreeable, especially with those in authority over us, or someone we want to impress, so if someone is smiling and nodding their head, they might just be being a pleasant listener. But when the eyebrows go up, you know they are really interested.

When I first had the concept for this book, it was about how to make change stick within an organization. When I talked to my clients about it, they smiled and thought it was cool, but when I changed the language to "this book is about three ways you can have less pain in growth mode," the eyebrows went up.

REFLECTING ON THE COURAGE TO EXPERIMENT

But What If It Sucks?

One of my favorite things is to take each of my sons on a one-on-one lunch every Saturday. I go for the connection and conversation and they, of course, go for the food. All three of them have their go-to restaurants that they rely on when it is their Saturday for lunch with Mom.

One Saturday, I suggested to Dillon, the youngest, that we try a new Asian place. He replied, "But, what if it sucks?" and I said "What if it doesn't? What if all this time we've been going to Pei Wei when the best Asian food in the world was right around the corner within walking distance? If we never try it, we'll never know!" What would you experiment with if you knew you couldn't fail? Could there be answers right around the corner that you are not trying?

(By the way, he was right: it *did* suck!)

Time to Think About Your Thinking!

Yes, let's reflect again! This time, we'll reflect on how you can have the courage to *experiment*.

1. How and where are you already using a more exper-imental mindset? Reflect on a few times this has worked for you and what you've learned from it.

a. Experimenting with curiosity:

_____

_____

b. Experimenting with a new approach:

_____

_____

c. Experimenting with testing:

_____

_____

2. In this chapter, there were more than 20 ideas and examples of how leaders like you chose to have the courage to experiment. Which concepts resonated with you? What could you do to be more experimental?

_____

_____

3. From those ideas, list the actions that you will take.

_____

_____

4. What might get in your way of doing those things this week? Hint: This is where the fear sneaks in!

_____

_____

5. How will you overcome those obstacles? Hint: "Just do it" is not a long-term strategy. Think about *who* can help, *what* resources you need, etc.

_____

_____

6. Based on your answers to the above questions, is there anything you could do next quarter or next year? Write it here so you can come back to it. There are no unrealistic goals, only unrealistic time frames. What can you get started on next week?

_____

_____

COURAGE AND CONFIDENCE

One of my superpowers is that I am regularly able to stand in awe of things. I cherish moments in nature when I get to witness what I call *perfect imperfection.* In my opinion, the mind is the most incredible thing to observe.

As I've been writing this book, my mind has been drawn to endless examples of how these Courage Mindsets work together. They can interrelate in so many ways to produce powerful, joyful results for the people who choose to use them. The three mindsets support each other. One is not more important than the other, nor do you need to have one to embrace the other. So, I'm going to leave you with one final thinking exercise to help the concepts sink in.

Courage gives you the confidence to leap toward progress. The mindset helps you stay there.

Now that you have learned how to alter your mindset as you lead your company, living in courage won't be a daily decision or a struggle; it will begin to feel normal. As I've coached courageous entrepreneurs and their leadership teams in various stages of their evolution, I've witnessed their confidence levels rise and their excitement increase. It becomes a virtuous cycle of increased courage and confidence. As you think courageously, you'll have more confidence in your actions.

Ask yourself...

- Am I committed to being courageously disciplined? Will I be in control of my time, my commitments, and my thoughts?

- Am I committed to being courageously lighthearted? Will I prioritize keeping the company positive in our reflections, the words we use, and the space that we energize?

- Am I committed to courageously experimenting with curiosity, new approaches, and testing instead of declaring?

I've witnessed time and time again that when my clients lead with these courageous mindsets, their greatest achievements are on the other side of the fear they leave behind. They learn to use the fear as a sign that they are ready to grow again. They learn to expand beyond the fear, and I know you can too. It's what you were designed for. Expect adversity, for there is no sure thing in the call to this entrepreneurial adventure, then let the courage lead you to boldness. Courage has magic, power, and genius in it!

I can't wait to see what your next courageous move will be!

For more Courage Advantage goodies,
visit JillYoung.com!

ACKNOWLEDGMENTS

A single page in the back of the book hardly seems fitting to express how appreciative I am to the ambitious people I get to be with every day, so hopefully I get to express it in person as well, soon. :)

Without clients who let me use their stories and served as test readers, this book would not exist. Thank you for being vulnerable and allowing me to share your story with other entrepreneurs so their journey can be a little more fun. We are all in this together.

Big thanks to:

My coaching network: These fine human beings are *masters* of their craft, and I'm so blessed to be surrounded by their knowledge and inspiration on a daily basis.

My support team: Lindsey, Stephanie, Maddie, Leslie, and Shana. You surprise me every day with your talents.

My family of boys: James, Brandon, Tyler, and Dillon. I often thought of you as I was writing this book, in hopes that it will help you live in courage someday!

Steve Chandler: For your lighthearted and simple approach to coaching and creativity.

Gino Wickman: For the human that you are and for the superhuman feat of creating EOS®.

Dan Sullivan: For your brilliant and consistent teachings on how an entrepreneur thinks and expands their freedom.

Brian Johnson: For doing all the heavy lifting with ancient wisdom and distilling it into one-minute lessons for your ADD friends!

And to Thor, the God of Thunder…just to see if anyone really reads the acknowledgments page! :)

RESEARCH NOTES

Proactive Training Saves Time and Money

HR Magazine reports that companies investing $1,500 or more per employee per year on training average 24% higher profit margins than companies with lower yearly training investments.

The American Society for Training and Development (ASTD) collected training information from over 2,500 firms and found that companies that offer comprehensive training:

1. Have 218% higher income per employee than those with less comprehensive training.

2. Enjoy a 24% higher profit margin than those who spend less on training, and

3. Generate a 6% higher shareholder return if the training expenditure per employee increases by $680.

For those who remain unconvinced, IBM provides yet another potent example. The international firm recently did a study to examine the percentage of capabilities that companies lose over time. When internal and external turnover, new technology and changes in businesses were factored in, the results were staggering. The study found that a company loses 10% to 30% of its original capabilities every year. Within three years, each company loses 41% of its staff. By year six, only 24% remain. Any business that doesn't believe in training, evolving, and moving their people forward is paying a much steeper price than it realizes.

Why Push-ups Are *Awesome*!

The benefits of adding push-ups to your regular exercise program are endless, says Yujin Lim, a physiologist at Optimal Health Exercise Physiology. "You build strength and promote muscle growth in your triceps, shoulders and chest and—if performed correctly with neutral spinal alignment—push-ups also improve your core strength and endurance," he says.

Collective Wellness Group wellness director Dan Conn says bodyweight exercises also help prevent injuries. "All strength training has the benefit of increasing natural growth hormones in your body, which has been linked with anti-aging benefits and can help to protect your body against injury," he says.

The Courage Advantage

COURSE

A leadership team course that
fosters a courage-focused
mindset and culture

LIVE KEYNOTES & WORKSHOPS

The Courage Advantage: Staring Down the Fear of Moving to Mastery

In this four-hour workshop, leaders will discover

» how to identify where fear is active in their leadership role and their company culture

» a four-step map of the stages of courage and how each stage lulls us to stay there

» the action steps needed to move us closer to mastery of our fears

INTERACTIVE WORKSHOP: 4 HOURS
LIVE KEYNOTE: 60-90 MINUTES

Accountability Activator

This is a day-long workshop for company leaders in growth mode. During this workshop, we explore the mindsets it takes to be a boss who creates an accountability culture. After participating in the workshop, managers feel confident in their ability to activate the productivity

» on their team

» in their department

» or for the entire company.

Designed strictly for management, this session can be held with multiple companies in attendance or it can be customized for individual organizations.

INTERACTIVE WORKSHOP: 5-7 HOURS
LIVE KEYNOTE: 60-90 MINUTES

Get a Grip: Are You Running Your Company or
Is Your Company Running You?

This workshop provides an introduction to how to run your company on the Entrepreneurial Operating System (EOS).

INTERACTIVE WORKSHOP: 3 HOURS
LIVE KEYNOTE: 90 MINUTES

Sign up today at JillYoung.com!

The Entrepreneurial Operating System® (EOS) is a practical set of concepts and tools that have helped thousands of entrepreneurs reach their business goals and find success. Implementing EOS will help you and your leadership team get better at three things:

» **Vision**—Getting everyone in your organization on the same page with where you're going and how you plan to get there.

» **Traction®**—Instilling focus, discipline, and accountability throughout the company so everyone executes the company vision every single day.

» **Health**—Helping your leaders become a more cohesive, functional, leadership team who creates a healthy work environment.

What is it about EOS that makes it work so well in a small, growing business?

» **Built for Busy Entrepreneurs.** EOS consists of practical concepts and tools that can be easily applied in a fast-paced small business.

» **Holistic Model and Approach.** EOS doesn't treat symptoms; it offers a universal approach that strengthens the Six Key Components™ of your business.

» **Designed to Solve Issues Once and for All.** EOS takes you below the surface to create real, permanent change and obtain meaningful results.

» **Brings Focus, Discipline and Accountability.** With every member of your team accountable for appropriate goals and objectives, you'll get consistently better results.

Visit JillYoung.com to see if EOS is right for you.

THE EARNING ADVANTAGE

The Earning Advantage: 8 Tools You Need to Get Paid the Money You Want is a book that I wrote for you, the boss! It provides resources to tackle the challenge of employee requests for a salary increase.

The Earning Advantage removes the guesswork and provides a concrete solution. So, the next time someone asks you for a raise, try this: Say, "Wow, this is really good news! Please read this book and schedule a time to meet with me in two weeks to discuss it." Then hand them the book.

The employee will either engage with the tools to produce more, earn a raise, and become a rock star employee, or they won't come back at all. You can now separate your star performers from low-level achievers and know how to address each.

The Earning Advantage Course for Employees
This course is for those employees who have a lot of potential but need the tools to maximize it.

The Earning Advantage Course—Boss Edition
The course will help you identify your low and high performers so you can motivate them, encourage their productivity, and maximize their potential.

Sign up today at JillYoung.com!

OTHER BOOKS
BY JILL YOUNG

The Earning Advantage:

8 Tools You Need to Get Paid
the Money You Want

The Thinking Advantage:

4 Essential Steps Your Team
Needs to Cultivate
Collaboration, Leverage
Creative Problem-Solving, and
Enjoy Exponential Growth

JILL YOUNG

CPSIA information can be obtained
at www.ICGtesting.com
Printed in the USA
BVHW070442081021
618416BV00003B/9

9 781647 462819